MW01289140

Julia,

In all that you are doing, keep pushing. Don't stop. Map out what you are called to do and push toward your destination.

Many Blessings,
Pastor Joel Wope

S T E E R

Eight Practices to Drive Leadership

JOEL WAYNE

WESTBOW
PRESS®
A DIVISION OF THOMAS NELSON
& ZONDERVAN

Copyright © 2019 Joel Wayne.

All rights reserved. No part of this book may be used or reproduced by
any means, graphic, electronic, or mechanical, including photocopying,
recording, taping or by any information storage retrieval system
without the written permission of the author except in the case of
brief quotations embodied in critical articles and reviews.

Photo credit: J Photography of Grand Rapids, LLC

WestBow Press books may be ordered through booksellers or by contacting:

WestBow Press
A Division of Thomas Nelson & Zondervan
1663 Liberty Drive
Bloomington, IN 47403
www.westbowpress.com
1 (866) 928-1240

Because of the dynamic nature of the Internet, any web addresses or
links contained in this book may have changed since publication and
may no longer be valid. The views expressed in this work are solely those
of the author and do not necessarily reflect the views of the publisher,
and the publisher hereby disclaims any responsibility for them.

This book is a work of non-fiction. Unless otherwise noted, the author
and the publisher make no explicit guarantees as to the accuracy of
the information contained in this book and in some cases, names of
people and places have been altered to protect their privacy.

Any people depicted in stock imagery provided by Shutterstock are
models, and such images are being used for illustrative purposes only.
Certain stock imagery © Shutterstock.

Scripture quotations are from the ESV® Bible (The Holy Bible, English
Standard Version®), copyright © 2001 by Crossway, a publishing ministry
of Good News Publishers. Used by permission. All rights reserved.

ISBN: 978-1-9736-5090-4 (sc)
ISBN: 978-1-9736-5089-8 (hc)
ISBN: 978-1-9736-5091-1 (e)

Library of Congress Control Number: 2019900338

Print information available on the last page.

WestBow Press rev. date: 03/22/2019

CONTENTS

Introduction

My wife, Melissa, and I had four kids in seven years. When they were seven, five, three, and nine months—and after years of sleepless nights and thousands of diapers—we were beginning to sense a bit of freedom to explore the world together. We decided to take a family bike ride. I strapped the youngest to my chest (possibly a poor decision), and our three-year-old, Ashley, was in a bike seat attached to Melissa's bike. The others were on their own bikes. We were living the dream.

The adventure was going well—fresh wind, gentle breezes, sunshine, the whole bit. As we were ending our twenty-minute bike ride, we finally pulled back onto our street, and Melissa transitioned from the road to the sidewalk. But as she steered the bike toward the sidewalk, her front tire failed to hit the curb properly. The one-inch granite curb was just steep enough to force the tire to slide along the curb, rather than hitting it straight. Melissa and Ashley went flying. When the bike landed, Ashley was still strapped into the bike seat but lying on her side just inches from the concrete.

I jumped off of my bike to check on our three-year-old. She was okay. I then ran to my wife only to discover scrapes up and down her leg and the side of her body. It was as though she had slid across fifty feet of glass. For weeks Melissa dealt with raw flesh, bandages, and discomfort—all because her steering was off.

Steering is crucial. As leaders, we have a huge responsibility to steer ourselves, our organization, and even our family. Being slightly off course can create discomfort and strain for an organization or family and have devastating effects if not properly handled. Even when the fall is completely accidental, as with my wife, it still has an enormous impact.

Over the past twenty years, I've guided businesses and churches. Throughout those years, I have discovered many leaders don't always know how to articulate their destination. Some have gotten distracted, others have never gained the clarity to lead with excellence, and some are simply unmotivated. Regardless, many leaders have steered their organizations and families in an undesirable direction or held them in a mode of complacency. Some are fully aware of the lack of proper steering but are unwilling to change course for fear of obstacles that seem to lie ahead.

Do you feel it is time to steer your life, organization, or family in a new direction? Is it time to firmly take hold of your life and move in a more purposeful trajectory? Are you excited about how you are steering your family or organization? Are you eager for others to see what is taking place in the lives of those you influence?

As a leader, I encourage you to answer the following questions that may help you determine where you currently stand:

Do you believe what you do matters?

Who are you influencing?

Are you serving a greater purpose than yourself?

How are you influencing where others are going?

Are you helping others steer toward value and influence?

How do you feel after answering the previous questions? Do you have a desire to steer your organization in a new direction—or course-correct even slightly so you don't hit the curb?

This book invites you to begin the journey of discovering the privilege and joy of steering with purpose and value. As a person of faith, I am certain that courses can be altered. Whether you're recovering from years of poor decisions or even intense fear, I believe all things can be overcome. I believe the next chapter is yours to write. It is my hope this book will provide a bit of guidance to begin taking small steps in a new direction.

In this book, you'll discover simple practices for healthy leadership from all aspects of life—business, family, faith, and more. This is a no-nonsense attempt to tackle leadership. The intent is for you to spend a few minutes walking through each chapter and possibly sharing some of your thoughts with those around you. In order to best support you, this book is short and concise and will ask questions designed to help you move forward. I encourage you to answer the questions at the end of each chapter and then take immediate steps forward.

Each chapter comes from my years of experience leading people and a boatload of mistakes made along the way. When you take notes or discuss topics with those around you, don't hesitate to include both personal and professional areas. It's amazing how small moments, like a bike ride with the family, can teach you so much about steering your way through life.

Take ownership, display courage, and steer toward a greater purpose. *Let's go.*

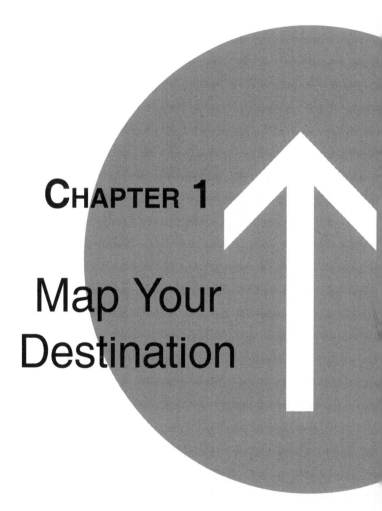

CHAPTER 1

Map Your Destination

If you cannot clearly communicate the role, purpose, and destination of your organization, you are cheating your organization and employees.

When I was called to be lead pastor at a church in the Midwest, I quickly found that it had not embraced its vision statement, and the staff was unsure of its goals. Amazing people of faith had come together to create a church, but there was no sign of a directional map for the organization. It is incredibly difficult and tiring to travel if you are not sure of your destination.

As we began our journey, we spent hours speaking about where we would invest time, energy, and resources. There were countless hours of prayer and dozens of giant sticky notes plastered on the meeting room walls. In the coming months, we discovered what our destination was going to be. It was exciting. Over the course of several months, we came together to put a metaphorical X on the map, and we decided to run hard to get there.

One significant and disheartening obstacle stood in the way. I likened the church to a four-door sedan. There is nothing wrong with sedans; I have owned some. However, the church decided that its destination would require them to get dirty. This meant we wanted to do anything necessary to help with and meet the needs of people around us. We were convinced we were called to go off road, to jump into the middle of a community, to partner with others, and to give more than 20 percent of our income to the local needs and missions. This also meant jumping into neighborhoods, schools, businesses, and government agencies. It meant challenging families at every level. It meant demonstrating the willingness to partner with marriages in times of crisis and times of joy.

We wanted to do all of this while growing a passionate leadership team from fewer than ten primary leaders to more than 150 adults who were engaged and passionate about where we were going. We wanted our purpose to sit in the hearts of all the leaders affecting their motivation and setting the course for others. For this to happen, we needed people to champion the vision, not simply memorize it.

It became clear to me that the four-door sedan was only going to take us so far. We needed a new vehicle. The sedan was efficient and cost-effective. It was fine for paved roads with only a few potholes, but our church had been called to go off road. We had been called to a greater purpose and vision than a small sedan could navigate. The terrain would be too difficult. Yes, modifications could help, but progress would be limited. Sometimes new tires and louder speakers just don't cut it.

So after several months of working together and getting clarity around our destination, we found ourselves in the market for a new vehicle. We needed to be ready to travel any type of terrain we encountered. We needed a jeep with knobby tires, off-road suspension, chassis clearance, roll bars, and four-wheel drive. We had to be ready to climb a mountain.

For some organizations, the new vehicle represents new hiring practices, greater expectations, realigning budgets, new processes, changing staff, and much more.

Two questions

First, do you know your destination? Your desired destination should be determined by how you believe your organization can influence others. You can begin by having core leaders call out key words to describe the current organization and what they hope it to be. Allow for the team around you to be honest or your travel plans will be hindered.

If you cannot clearly communicate the role, purpose, and destination of your organization, you are cheating your organization and employees.

It is called purpose and vision. People need to understand where they are going, not only where you don't want them to go. Where you place ultimate *value* leads to *passion*, and passion fosters *purpose*. Be determined to ensure that everyone is moving in the same direction. Yes, God can use you to do this.

> But for this purpose I have raised you up, to show you my power, so that my name may be proclaimed in all the earth.
>
> (Exodus 9:16)

Second, are you driving a vehicle that will allow you to get to your destination? All organizations are built differently, each with its own personality. You must determine if your current vehicle (structure of your organization) can allow you to accomplish all you've been called to do. This involves the organization at large, individual employees, and your leadership.

Difficult decisions will need to be made in order to assure that those around you are ready to get muddy. Hire people who *count the cost*. Do not hire people who count the cost of the hard work but who count the cost of failing to arrive at the chosen destination.

There is a cost to doing nothing. Please don't complain about your current condition if you're unwilling to make tough decisions and take action toward your destination. This means adding people to your team who add horsepower. People who value the destination and purpose of the organization add horsepower. Here's a quick caution: one of the greatest threats to your team is not people who recognizably give or take energy and power, but those who are dead weight. Be willing to honestly evaluate the amount of horsepower given by members of your team.

A clear plan and a clear destination matter. People without a clear understanding of their destination are easily distracted. You can be pulled toward objectives that limit your overall goal. Clearly map your destination. Throw it on mugs and on the wall of your conference room. Make sure your leadership team has memorized every word of the vision and is driving toward it.

Takeaway/Questions:

1. What is the primary purpose of your organization and/or family?

2. Based on your desired destination, do you have the correct vehicle for traveling?

3. Can you easily identify how each person adds horsepower in driving the organization toward its destination?

 Next Steps:

1. Write three goals for where you desire to be in six months, one year, and three years.

    six months:

    one year:

three years:

2. Creatively communicate your destination in writing and other creative ways to your team. Name three places where you will place the vision for the team to see.

    1.

    2.

    3.

CHAPTER 2

Lead Hard

When the hope of what you may gain for others is greater than the fear of what you may lose for yourself, you can become a great leader.

Three years. After three years, an organization is a reflection of its leadership. Vision, strategy, purpose, and culture all point in the direction of leadership. Why? Because leadership matters.

Jeff decided to purchase his parents' business. It was a significant purchase financially. It was also a risky purchase in terms of leadership. Jeff wanted the organization to keep its values but also had ideas about how to increase its footprint through new ventures and products. The initial transition went well, but after a few months, there was tension when he attempted to alter production and attitude.

Why was Jeff struggling? Why the tension? It wasn't a financial issue. The bank had completed a thorough financial review to ensure the business was in order. After several months of plugging in numbers and discussing succession planning, the contract was signed.

Jeff's biggest error? He gave little consideration to doing a leadership review. A review of leadership gives an accurate picture and accounting of the capacity and competency of an organization moving forward. People neglect this area because leadership and culture are often vastly undervalued.

In Jeff's case, the problem centered on a culture established by his parents, not by Jeff. The employees had grown accustomed to the way things were done and likely expected a family member to continue in the same vein. Jeff had planned on committing his time and energy to increasing sales and new products and acquiring new hires. Instead he found his time quickly fell to conducting day-to-day operations.

Jeff remained committed and was still pleased with his decision to purchase the business, but he knew his vision was crumbling under the vision he had inherited. His desires and plans created a bit of uneasiness for the employees. Time and energy were needed to determine the best way to steer the culture to not only accept but also embrace an altered direction.

Fortunately, after nearly two years of crafting the culture, people became excited about the upcoming journey.

> Where there is no guidance, a people falls, but
> in an abundance of counselors there is safety.
> (Proverbs 11:14)

People need leadership. However, people first buy into the leader who is setting the course. Leaders are to guide and direct others. If you are not embracing the destination you have set, do not expect others to do so. You are being naive and—even worse—a poor leader.

Jeff's story is a living example of someone willing to travel the long road of guiding others to a greater destination. The people were living and acting according to the destination set years before. Jeff needed to communicate his vision.

Leadership is tiring and often lonely. Leadership is more than pointing your finger toward a specific goal and telling everyone to "go there." It's more than delegating tasks. Leading well is empowering others with a clear purpose. Good leaders are hard to find and don't come cheap.

Healthy leadership alters the DNA. It gives confidence to others so they can make healthy decisions. It affects culture and even societies in profound ways. Excellent leaders are intentional. It is ingrained deep within some while able to be learned by others. When stepping into any organization or family, you are inheriting a culture that must be influenced through leadership.

Leadership can steer an organization or family from frustration and hostility to encouragement and purpose.

Your leadership is your motor. Like with a speedboat, the power of your motor creates the wake that carries your impact to distant shorelines. The size of the wake determines the impact you can have. Make sure you have the correct motor in place to ensure you are allowing your leadership to run at its best.

As a leader, you are always steering organizational culture in some capacity. The culture of family, business, friends, church, sports, and the like are all being steered. Granted, some leaders have steered culture into a sinkhole of undelivered promises or an abyss of unclear goals and objectives. Others have steered the culture into an unforeseen strength that stands in the center of severe adversity and seems to relish a challenge, knowing there is a strong team ready to weather the storm.

Some have inherited a particular culture that feels as though the previous leadership was steered into the depth of mediocrity, while others have inherited a culture that seems to ooze poison and hostility. Regardless, the ship can be turned. The house can be rebuilt.

By the way, many things can serve as obstacles in turning a ship. In a later chapter, I refer to them as "splinters." However, consider for a moment the following thought.

Mature leadership invites accountability.

Read it again: mature leadership invites accountability. This requires humility. Ask those around you how they think things are going. Ask how they would improve or possibly change the way their given areas of responsibility are handled. Ask if they believe leadership is reflecting the purpose and destination that has been communicated. Too many times leadership is unwilling to evaluate the changes *they* need to make. Wow, this is hard. But it can be done.

Takeaway/Questions:

1. Leadership demands consistency and trust. Where am I inconsistent or untrustworthy?

2. Identify the reasons you are struggling to be more intentional with your leadership. Are you facing opposition, or does it feel too hard?

3. How are my top leaders and I functioning as motors? Are we creating impactful wake?

 Next Steps:

1. Be vulnerable, and invite someone to hold you accountable for leading with excellence and modeling your organization's purpose.

2. Name a person you can sit down with in the coming weeks to speak about being a mentor to you in leadership.

CHAPTER 3

Shifting Culture

**The culture you build reveals
what you value most.**

The first time I went to Uganda I was astonished by the landscape. The smells, sounds, and tastes were new to me. As we drove on the opposite side of the road and watched zebras run, I found amazing people who were kind and generous. It was in Uganda that I also discovered my first banana plant— something that certainly doesn't grow in the Midwest. Bananas in Uganda were a bit different from what I was accustomed to: shorter, sweeter, and denser in consistency.

As my senses took in this new banana experience, I became curious about why bananas are curved. Do you know why? It has to do with geotropism: the growth of the parts of plants with respect to the force of gravity. The upward growth of plant shoots is an instance of negative geotropism (growing against gravity toward its food source); the downward growth of roots is positive geotropism (growing with gravity toward its food source). Bananas are curved because, despite the pull of gravity, they grow upward toward the sun.

Organizations and businesses are similar in that they, too, bend toward whatever impacts or feeds them the most. Influencing (or feeding) your organization or area of leadership is based on many motivations and can be done in a variety of ways, not just through monetary rewards. Things that positively shape culture can include incentives, bonuses, and customer service, or sending a note of appreciation, performing an act of kindness, or simply serving someone in need. Many organizations thrive because of their desire to serve. It's a powerful quality that starts with leadership and spreads through the entire organization.

It shall not be so among you. But whoever would be great among you must be your servant.

(Matthew 20:26)

Negative or detrimental acts of feeding your culture could be backstabbing, gossip, low expectations, poor communication, fear and intimidation, and similar areas. Of course, this kind of "feeding" actually starves your people of the very things they need: a sense of purpose at work and opportunities to grow. As leaders, we have the opportunity to influence and inspire our organization and the culture as a whole, and our words and actions will cause people to either bend positively or negatively.

A dictionary will tell you that culture is a set of shared attitudes and values. This makes the leader's task of setting the culture both simple and complex, but the exciting opportunity for leaders is recognizing that building a strong culture can set the foundation for positivity, productivity, and efficiency—all things that can absolutely change the trajectory of a business.

Building a strong culture can dominate the landscape of an industry and even steer a society in a new direction.

I like to encourage leaders to begin meetings by allowing others to share positive experiences, sometimes called "wins" or "victories," from the previous week. Set a timer, and allow a few people to share. You don't need to share for more than five minutes, but this simple act gives you the opportunity to encourage others, and in doing so, it allows others to see what is most important to you. Landing a new account, increased engagement, or a new hire can all be wins.

Perhaps you have heard the saying "You celebrate what you value and value what you celebrate." It's true. Take time to appreciate and acknowledge the wins. Give some thought to how you can create traditions, such as recognizing someone at a weekly stand-up meeting. It doesn't have to be big or involve handing out trophies, but these moments can give a team needed energy and perseverance to keep running during times of difficulty. A few examples of victories would be new clients, increased sales, an employee who shows great character, or serving the community together.

Building culture won't happen overnight, but being intentional in your efforts will eventually pay off. Here are some things you can do now to move the needle: Feed your people healthy food. Never take credit for yourself. Build up others. Serve people with excellence. Value the right things. It takes consistency and inner grit to steer culture to do great things, but it is achievable, and it is worth it.

Where and how are you steering culture? Are you willing to answer honestly? *Leaders drive culture.* If you don't like what is happening, look in the mirror and keep reading. We'll address a component of culture in each chapter of this book.

Takeaway/Questions:

1. What is feeding your team?

2. What is the biggest thing causing your team to bend and curve right now?

3. Have you created a healthy culture?

4. What are the important components of a healthy culture?

 Next Steps:

List three components of negative culture within your organization or family.

1.

2.

3.

Now list two ways you can work to start bending them in a positive direction within the next three months.

1.

2.

CHAPTER 4

Keep Your Motivation

The ability to keep your motivation can hinge on whether your destination serves a greater purpose than just yourself.

On the wall in my office hangs a three-foot sword with an etched inscription that reads, "I am doing a great work and I cannot come down." It's from the book of Nehemiah, chapter 6, verse 3. On the other side of the sword are the names of the pastors and elders with whom I have had the honor of serving. The sword was a gift, and I treasure it greatly. It is a powerful reminder of what can happen when a group of people moves together in the same direction. In the midst of change, transition, and hardship, we have learned what it means to stand together as a team. The sword also serves as a reminder of the destination. It serves to motivate me in running toward the X on the map. When thinking of the team around me, I am infused with courage and confidence to step forward toward our destination, regardless of the hardship.

As leaders, we must stay motivated and focused because our end goal matters. If the end goal isn't great, our purpose and destination aren't big enough.

If you have a small goal, you'll likely have little motivation. With a bigger purpose comes greater motivation.

Some people seem to relish "living in the overwhelmed." Leaders can run toward one objective while simultaneously moving toward another. Be careful. Running hard and fast is great, but you must not leave those around you confused about where the organization's energy and passion should be directed. The need for clarity is hugely important.

As humans, we were meant to be pushed. However, the real challenge often begins when you feel defeated. You feel that you have been broken physically, mentally, emotionally, and spiritually. You're done. You don't desire to move forward because you don't feel like you have the strength or the stamina. You live in the pain of failure and bear the scars of regret. A crumbling relationship, overwhelming debt, a dead-end career, or a poor decision can absolutely drain your motivation and will to carry on. But those are the times you have to remember that when you overcome the most difficult of times, you can gain the most.

The greatest obstacle in making an unprecedented journey of courage is fear.

I remember moving to lead a congregation in Kentucky. We were excited to be closer to our family, but the move exposed some vulnerabilities (fear, doubt, and lack of preparedness). Those moments forced me to rest in my faith. Ironically, vulnerabilities are tied to the beauty that lies at the center of trust and faith. Staring down your vulnerabilities and returning to the solid foundation of faith is an eloquent yet vicious cycle believers should explore—especially if they are leaders. Why? Genuine leadership requires vulnerability. The leader sees the risk and possible conflict with greater clarity than others. Thus the need for great faith and great trust.

> Have I not commanded you? Be strong and courageous. Do not be frightened, and do not be dismayed, for the LORD your God is with you wherever you go.
>
> (Joshua 1:9)

Takeaway/Questions:

1. What scars are limiting your motivation?

2. What is your greatest fear in accomplishing your purpose?

 Next Steps:

1. Resolve to set aside the past and fear of failure and live in faith, knowing God is going to use you for a great work.

2. Commit time daily to work toward your goals listed in chapter 1.

CHAPTER 5

Establishing Default Settings

"

Creating and building
healthy default settings
is a crucial aspect of
establishing a healthy
culture with lasting impact.

"

One of the most popular movies of my childhood was *Top Gun*. If you have any recollection of what that movie was about, you can envision two aircraft pilots giving a high five and then throwing their arms downward, their hands hitting again around their hip. It was beyond cool. From that point on, it seemed as though every high school basketball team, college football player, professional athlete, and action star had a special handshake.

My wife and I have passed that tradition to our children. Each one of them has helped craft a good-night handshake with each of the other family members. We had no idea the amount of energy that would be needed to implement such chaos at bedtime. It has become ingrained in our children's normal routine. Without it, we can have children unable to go to sleep. Why? Because over the years, they have adopted it as a default setting. It is similar, but not as important, as saying a prayer with each child in the evening. It is something they are so accustomed to that without it, their nightly routine is disrupted.

Yes, special handshakes are a silly example, but the illustration is relevant. Everyone has default settings or routines that impact their lives on a daily basis.

It's similar within organizations. All organizations have default settings. People naturally return to that which they have grown most accustomed. When stressed, some people turn to food, and others exercise or even throw money at the problem. When overworked, some become short-tempered or make poor decisions. When hungry, some people become "hangry."

> **Healthy default settings recalibrate the temperature of an organization, providing comfort and assurance during difficulty and an awareness that you are working toward something bigger than the individual.**

For the church I pastor, prayer is a default setting. In times of confusion, stress, or the unknown, we frequently call a three-minute huddle for everyone to come together and look each other in the eyes, remembering that the call is always greater than one person. Then we say a brief prayer.

The work remains, but shoulders immediately loosen and smiles return. Healthy default settings can change your view: what was once a crisis is now seen as a challenge to be overcome. Default settings ground you. Default settings allow you to move your eyes beyond yourself and look to others.

Your default settings need to be woven into the organizational DNA. Here are some possible default settings you can begin to implement with your team:

- Remember the destination.
- Clarify the objectives.
- Always be willing to smile.
- Put others first.

- Hold a stand-up meeting for open communication.
- Celebrate wins together.

Commit your work to the LORD, and your plans will be established.

(Proverbs 16:3)

Takeaway/Questions:

1. When things become stressful, how do you respond? How does your company respond?

2. What are your organization's default settings?

3. What characteristics do you want people to remember when thinking of your company? Or of your leadership?

 Next Steps:

1. Send an anonymous survey asking others what they think is most important to the organization.

2. Think of two positive default settings that would make an impact on your organization's functions.

CHAPTER 6

Building Expectations

"

Healthy expectations
allow for greater clarity,
leading to more consistent
productivity and a higher
sense of ownership.

My childhood was shaped by the tall pines, red dirt, and humid air of southern Alabama. I spent many summer evenings playing with friends until the sun set and the stars twinkled. But some of my favorite memories happened while walking behind my father as he pushed a tiller through a half-acre garden. He would use the tiller to make parallel passes forming rows in the soil. I'll never forget the day he told me it was my turn. He had already tilled a couple of rows and then he handed the tiller to me. He gave me a few instructions, telling me to keep it straight and to stop if I began to stray out of line.

I was ready. This was going to be a boy's step into manhood. I finally had the opportunity to show my father how strong I had become—but things didn't go as planned. I quickly began losing "the line" my father started, and when looking behind at the job I had done, well, it looked like a wet noodle coming out of boiling water.

My father quickly corrected the trajectory, telling me to keep it straight. My comment: "Dad, I was off just a little." He told me that if not corrected, that small mistake would mean that the garden would be a mess. I knew his expectation. It is one illustration that was typically followed by words like "everything you do says something about you."

As leaders, we let too many things slide because we are tired or don't have the courage to cope with correcting someone or something. We lose sight of our destination. Focus is deterred and caution ignored if not kept before the leader. A leader keeps everyone moving in the proper direction, knowing that uncorrected errors multiply.

A leader must communicate clear expectations in order for others to perform at their best.

No one wants to be evaluated for something they didn't know was expected. Developing clear and concise expectations benefit both employee and employer. I have encountered numerous people who have been corrected for walking in a "crooked line" without ever being told what a straight line is. That is poor leadership.

Face it, most employees are graded in terms of fulfilling expectations, not a job description. To grade without clear expectations leads to a lack of trust and respect.

Benefits of healthy expectations for the employer:

- Less time spent micromanaging
- More likely to get a productive employee
- Easier to evaluate if the person is serving in the proper role
- Able to determine if their role can be incorporated elsewhere

Benefits of healthy expectations for the employee:

- Greater confidence in the employer
- Greater confidence in his or her own abilities

- Greater productivity by prioritizing energy and time
- Greater clarity that leads to job satisfaction and empowerment

And let us not grow weary of doing good, for in due season we will reap, if we do not give up.

(Galatians 6:9)

Takeaway/Questions:

1. What does clarity look like to you?

2. Have you communicated clear expectations?

3. Would your people agree that you are clear enough?

 Next Steps:

1. Write down the five primary expectations you have for yourself.

2. Work with your people to establish what it means to be a good member of your team.

3. Work with your family to establish five primary expectations for what it means to be a good member of the family.

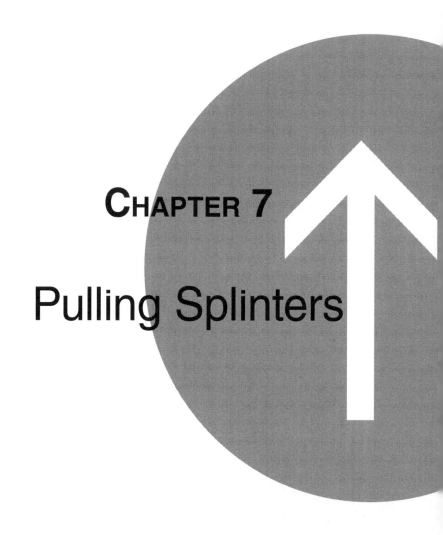

Chapter 7

Pulling Splinters

Recognizing and dealing with splinters within your organization prevents irritation and frustration.

I was chasing my two-year-old across our back deck. As I rounded the corner, I rubbed my hand across the top rail, feeling several splinters slide into my fingers. I slowly pulled them out, failing to recognize one that had buried a bit deeper into my thumb. Two days later, I could tell by the tenderness that it had quickly become infected. Hoping it would grow out of my skin on its own, I ignored it. Within a few days, it was in full-on infection mode, impacting the way that I worked and how I was playing with my children.

This is indicative of our lives for many of us. We end up with small splinters that lead to discomfort and conflict. Yet we fail to cope or deal with them appropriately. They fester, eventually becoming infected, all because we would not take the time to deal with them properly when they initially happened.

Many leaders hold in their frustrations and have mental conflicts with others while outwardly pretending all is well. In time, productivity, team chemistry, the longevity of employees, and revenue are all impacted.

The struggle is two-fold: identifying splinters and knowing how to cope with them.

> If possible, so far as it depends on you, live
> peaceably with all.
> (Romans 12:18)

Many of us fear confrontation, but without confrontation, wounds will fester. When there are genuine problems in the body, we have a responsibility to begin the process of healing by confronting the issue.

The greatest splinter is a poor attitude.

Splinters often not identified:

- Someone with a poor attitude
- People who don't know what is expected and lack clarity
- Another leader who tries to assume your responsibility
- Someone with a lack of purpose due to little direction/vision
- Someone who pulls with less strength than the rest of the team
- People who take credit for everything
- People who grumble and complain (negativity)

Coping with splinters:
The primary reason for not coping with conflict is fear. *Talk* about your splinters. Coping with splinters is hard for most because it is rarely done. Frequency allows for easier conversations, creating an environment of expected improvement with little room for passive-aggressive personalities.

Preventing splinters:
Having practices in place to quickly deal with splinters and avoid unnecessary difficulty is always in the best interest of the organization. Implementing the following practices will help alleviate stress, save money, and create a healthier environment for everyone:

- Write out and clearly define expectations for positions and roles.

- Plan times to address splinters (no one wants to be surprised).
- Don't buy into "negative talk" (the Bible calls this gossip and slander).

A secondary source of splinters is a lack of awareness. You don't understand the damage done by not confronting a difficult situation. Something that seemed minor can quickly become major. Coping with splinters is an opportunity to grow, mature, and influence others to do the same.

Takeaway/Questions:

1. Splinters get infected if not removed and show up in our lives as unresolved conflict.

2. What splinters do you currently have both personally and professionally?

3. What steps are you willing to take in the next week to address a splinter?

 Next Steps:

Schedule regular meetings (five to ten minutes) with other leaders to clearly identify any splinters.

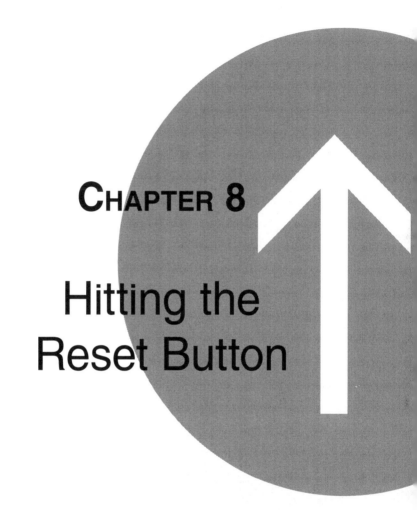

CHAPTER 8

Hitting the
Reset Button

**Hitting the reset button
can mean releasing the
old and chasing the new.**

When my oldest son, Carson, was five years old, it was time for him to start kindergarten. The school was just one block from our home, and we would go there as a family to play on the playground regularly. In other words, the place was familiar to him.

However, the first day of kindergarten came, and my son was nervous. In fact, my wife packed up the other kids to make the walk to the school, and Carson was determined he wasn't going.

Melissa tried to scoot him out the door, but he grabbed on to the doorframe with fingers of fury and dug his feet into the ground. Melissa started to pull, but my son simply held on tighter, refusing to let go. Carson was determined to stay home, and he began screaming and crying, "I won't go!" Finally, Melissa pried off each finger one by one and carried him down the street to school.

I sat in a meeting as these events unfolded. The continual ringing of my cell phone gave reason to answer. Melissa informed me of the events of the morning, and I left work to go meet her at school. Carson was not happy; in fact, he was having a complete meltdown. I picked him up in my arms and tried to force him into his class. Again he grabbed the doorframe. I am convinced he had biblical strength (think Samson with hair). His fingers locked onto the frame, and his strength was staggering.

Many of us have held on to doorframes in our lives because we simply could not tolerate the thought of change. Fear grips our heart, and we fail to recognize the growth that could come with change.

For many leaders, the fear is real. Perhaps you experience inner angst simply thinking about how others will respond to change. Additionally, many have fallen into the rut of a daily routine of monotonous work that we seemingly cannot get out of. One difficulty of leading change and growth is the daily intentionality needed to move forward. Although it can sting a bit, we need to rip off the proverbial adhesive bandage rather than pull slowly. We need to hit "reset."

Wouldn't it be great to have a large red button we could hit that read "reset"? Sometimes we need to reset our organization. Likewise, sometimes leaders need to look at others and say, "Hey, guys, this is going okay, but we have been called to do much more, and I want us to do some things differently. Don't worry; it is going to start with me. But we are going to put signs all over the place reminding us of our destination. We are going to establish default settings that keep us focused and motivated. Each person is going to build five key expectations for his or her position, which will be used in a review process so we move forward and remove the splinters that are hindering us. It will be hard but well worth it."

If you can't tell, I have said that a few times.

But it is worth it. Why? Because as much as our default is to cling to the doorframes of change, yelling in protest, the majority of people simply need to know they will be supported and encouraged in the midst of change.

What causes the need to hit the reset button?

- Giving voice to the wrong people
- Losing focus
- Using the wrong tools (like trying to dig a swimming pool with a spoon)

Questions to help determine the need for a reset:

- Does customer care take a back seat?
- Is an agenda being pushed that doesn't move toward the vision of the organization?
- Are you frustrated with the drama among colleagues?
- Do you detest mediocrity in your organization?
- Have you lost the passion from when you began?
- Do you desire to see an organization do more than you have ever imagined, regardless of how far it has previously come?

> **It takes grit to hit the reset button. Not a little. A lot. The kind of grit that wakes you up in the middle of the night.**

You need an inner determination to be an instrumental part of building a culture that leads and guides an organization to chase excellence in every aspect. But, it is evident when a leader has the depth of determination and humility needed to push an organization forward.

It will be evident by seeing a clear destination and vision that has crept into every crack of the organization. An intentional strategy propels the organization with purpose. Leaders within the organization begin to model the company's vision; employees find value and worth in giving of their time and talents; clients and customers are inspired to reflect your organization in their own lives.

This endeavor of change and growth will always begin with core leadership. As a leader, meet with the primary leadership team regularly, getting all team members on the same page. It doesn't have to take a large amount of time. In ten minutes, you can communicate passion, add direction, and give encouragement.

Quick Tip: Use a timer. I have been known to use an egg timer to keep things purposeful and moving efficiently. This allows for effective use of time for the individual and the organization.

Note: If the primary leader has given you the responsibility of steering culture, make sure he or she fully supports the movement, and you have been given both the responsibility and the authority. Clearly let the primary leader know what you are doing and what you are going to implement.

> Remember not the former things, nor consider the things of old. Behold, I am doing a new thing; now it springs forth, do you not perceive it? I will make a way in the wilderness and rivers in the desert.
> (Isaiah 43:18–19)

Takeaway/Questions:

1. What areas of your organization or family need to be reset?

2. What behaviors are you seeing that tell you it's time to reset?

 Next Steps:

Write down three things you would like to be changed in your organization or family, and share them with someone you trust.

1.

2.

3.

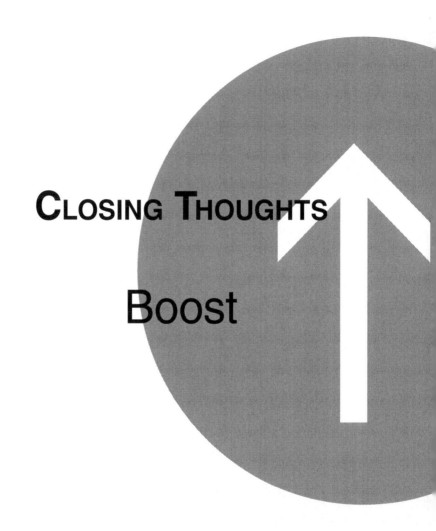

Closing Thoughts

Boost

It was my first, and only, marathon. I previously ran a half marathon and determined a full race couldn't be much different. I trained with my longest run at seventeen miles. I don't think it registered with me that a marathon was an additional 9.2 miles.

I woke early on race day and made my way to the start. Both half marathoners and marathoners were put in the same corrals before the race, according to estimated run time. I quickly realized that the majority of runners were doing the half marathon, and the courses split from one another around mile eleven. I started strong, sticking to a predetermined game plan and pace. Before I knew it, I came to the intersection where the marathoners and half marathoners split from one another. The road came to an end. Two large signs dominated the landscape. One read "Half Marathoners," with a large arrow pointing to the left. The other, "Marathoners," had an arrow pointing to the right. As I got closer, I noticed that no one was going right on the marathon path, which I was to take. Seriously, *no one* was going right. I started to think some teenage punk messed with the sign. Regardless, I turned right.

In the span of thirty seconds, I went from running among dozens of other runners to jogging down a four-lane road through the middle of a large city, waiting for tumbleweeds to cross the road. My spirits immediately deflated. How could I run another fifteen miles alone? Fortunately, after a few minutes, I came upon a couple of other runners, and a few caught up to me from behind. My spirits lifted slightly, but I had to fight mental fatigue.

This is leadership. At times, you are cruising along, doing all that you had planned. Other times, you are alone and experience serious mental, emotional, and spiritual fatigue. You question if it is worth the journey. It is actually a little humorous. You can prepare for months and then contemplate quitting because of a few moments of feeling alone. Silly, yes, but it is still a reality.

Fortunately, I did not stop running the race. I kept going.

I am asking you not to stop. Remember what your destination is and keep fighting. **Do *not* stop running**. Never give up.

REMEMBER THAT WHICH YOU HAVE BEEN CALLED TO DO AND YOUR DESTINATION.

When they know the destination, people run harder.

LEAD WELL AND WITH PURPOSE.

You can change an organization
and even a future generation.

BUILD A HEALTHY CULTURE.

A healthy culture can provide the needed courage to do the audacious.

STAY MOTIVATED TO DO SOMETHING GREATER THAN YOURSELF.

What you are running toward is too big for only you.

ESTABLISH DEFAULT SETTINGS.

Tell those around you the values
you will not abandon.

ESTABLISH CLEAR EXPECTATIONS FOR OTHERS THAT BUILD TO THE DESTINATION (VISION).

Empower your team to run with clarity.

HAVE THE COURAGE TO
DEAL WITH SPLINTERS.

Handling conflict can be the greatest
opportunity to increase your voice.

WHEN NEEDED, HAVE THE HUMILITY TO HIT "RESET."

This gives value to the work at hand.

Don't give up.

You can't bypass endurance to know true courage.

There is no healthy precedent in the Bible for giving up. The road can be long and exasperating, but you can endure. Don't give in. Don't give up. God is faithful.

**And remember,
it's *never* too late to be who
God created you to be.**

I have fought the good fight, I have finished the race, I have kept the faith.

(2 Timothy 4:7)

ABOUT THE AUTHOR

Joel Wayne has spent twenty years improving leadership and cultivating healthy culture within organizations and churches in Connecticut, Kentucky, and Michigan. He currently serves as lead pastor for Chapel Pointe in Michigan and is founder of VSI Leadership, a business and leadership consulting group. Joel's dynamic communication style conveys his enthusiasm for developing strong leaders focusing on VISION, STRATEGY, and IMPLEMENTATION to create an overall organizational reset. He currently lives in Michigan with his wife and four children.

Find out more about Joel Wayne:
www.joelcwayne.com

PGdL2016USA